Hymns FOR THE Master

15 FAVORITE HYMNS FOR SOLO PERFORMANCE

Arranged by Stan Pethel

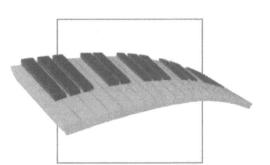

This book is designed to be used with the following solo books:

00841136	Flute	00841139	Trumpet
00841137	Clarinet	00841140	Trombone
00841138	Alto Sax		

ISBN 978-0-7935-8608-0

HAL•LEONARD®
CORPORATION
7777 W. BLUEMOUND RD. P.O. BOX 13819 MILWAUKEE, WI 53213

Visit Hal Leonard Online at
www.halleonard.com

ALL CREATURES OF OUR GOD AND KING

Words by Francis of Assisi
Music by Geistliche Kirchengesang

broaden to end

rit.

rit.

Ped.

ALL HAIL THE POWER OF JESUS' NAME

Words by Edward Perronet
Music by Oliver Holden

AMAZING GRACE

Words by John Newton
Music by Virginia Harmony

With simplicity

BE THOU MY VISION

Traditional Irish

CROWN HIM WITH MANY CROWNS

Words by Matthew Bridges
Music by George Job Elvey

FOR THE BEAUTY OF THE EARTH

Text by Folliot S. Pierpont
Music by Conrad Kocher

Moderately

GOD OF GRACE AND GOD OF GLORY

Text by Harry Emerson Fosdick
Music by John Hughes

I LOVE THEE

Traditional

JESUS SHALL REIGN WHERE'ER SUN

Words by Isaac Watts
Music by John Hatton

JOYFUL, JOYFUL WE ADORE THEE

Words by Henry van Dyke
Music by Ludwig Van Beethoven, melody from Ninth Symphony
Adapted by Edward Hodges

MY FAITH LOOKS UP TO THEE

Words by Ray Palmer
Music by Lowell Mason

SAVIOR LIKE A SHEPHERD LEAD US

Words attributed to Dorothy A. Thrupp
Music by William B. Bradbury

THIS IS MY FATHER'S WORLD

Words by Maltbie Babcock
Music by Franklin L. Sheppard

WHEN I SURVEY THE WONDROUS CROSS

Words by Lowell Mason
Music by Isaac Watts

TAKE MY LIFE AND LET IT BE

Words by Frances R. Havergal
Music by Louis J.F. Herold, Arranged by George Kingsley